D0100427

SPACE FACTS AND FIGURES

ASTEROIDS, METEORS, AND COMETS

Nancy Dickmann

WINDMILL
BOOKS

Published in 2019 by **Windmill Books**, an imprint of Rosen Publishing
29 East 21st Street, New York, NY 10010

Copyright © 2019 BROWN BEAR BOOKS LTD

All rights reserved. No part of this book may be reproduced in any form
without permission in writing from the publisher, except by a reviewer.

For Brown Bear Books Ltd:
Text and Editor: Nancy Dickmann
Children's Publisher: Anne O'Daly
Editorial Director: Lindsey Lowe
Design Manager: Keith Davis
Designer and Illustrator: Supriya Sahai
Picture Manager: Sophie Mortimer

Concept development: Square and Circus/Brown Bear Books Ltd

Picture Credits:
Front cover: Supriya Sahai
Interior: iStock: bjdizx 23; NASA: 13, 19, ESA/Rosetta/MPS for OSIRIS Team MPS/UPD/LAM/
IAA/SSO/INTA/UPM/DASP/IDA 14, 20, 28, JPL 7, 9 16, 21, 29t, JPL-Caltech 8, JPL/M. Showalter
18, JPL/UMD 16–17; Shutterstock: 3DMI 26bc, 29b, Marcel Clemens 15, 26bl, Coldmoon
Photoproject 26br, John A. Davis 10, Oliver Denker 11, Melkor3D 4, Mopic 6, 24, Dmitry P
ichugin 27, Vadim Sadovski 22, Marc Ward 25.

Key: t=top, b=bottom, c=center, l=left, r=right

Brown Bear Books has made every attempt to contact the copyright holder.
If anyone has any information please contact licensing@brownbearbooks.co.uk

Cataloging-in-Publication Data

Names: Dickmann, Nancy.
Title: Asteroids, meteors, and comets / Nancy Dickmann.
Description: New York : Windmill Books, 2019. | Series: Space facts and figures |
Includes glossary and index.
Identifiers: LCCN ISBN 9781508195078 (pbk.) | ISBN 9781508195061 (library bound) |
ISBN 9781508195085 (6 pack)
Subjects: LCSH: Asteroids--Juvenile literature. | Meteors--Juvenile literature. |
Comets--Juvenile literature.
Classification: LCC QB377.D53 2019 | DDC 523.4--dc23

Manufactured in the United States of America

CPSIA Compliance Information: Batch #BS18WM:
For Further Information contact Rosen Publishing, New York, New York at 1-800-237-9932

CONTENTS

Going Around the Sun 4

Asteroids 6

Vesta 8

Near-Earth Asteroids 10

Eros 12

Comets 14

Inside a Comet 16

Comet Shoemaker-Levy 18

Rosetta 20

Meteors 22

Meteor Showers 24

Meteorites 26

Quiz 28

Glossary 30

Further Resources 31

Index 32

GOING AROUND THE SUN

Our solar system is made up of millions of objects that travel around the sun. Some are big, and others are smaller.

The eight planets are some of the largest objects in the **solar system**. Smaller rocks are called asteroids. There are millions of them. Comets are made of ice and dust. They travel around the sun in long, looping paths, with their long tails streaming out. These objects often crash into **moons** and planets—including Earth. Space rocks that land on Earth are called **meteorites**.

Craters on Earth's moon and other space objects were caused by comets or asteroids crashing into them.

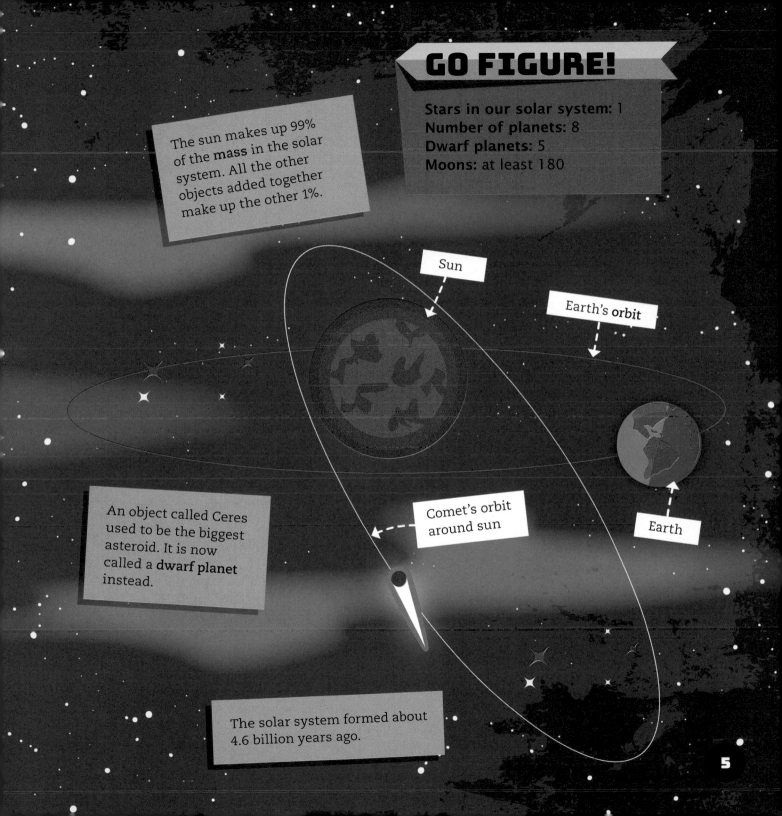

GO FIGURE!

Stars in our solar system: 1
Number of planets: 8
Dwarf planets: 5
Moons: at least 180

The sun makes up 99% of the **mass** in the solar system. All the other objects added together make up the other 1%.

Sun

Earth's **orbit**

An object called Ceres used to be the biggest asteroid. It is now called a **dwarf planet** instead.

Comet's orbit around sun

Earth

The solar system formed about 4.6 billion years ago.

ASTEROIDS

Asteroids are rocky lumps that go around the sun. They are too small to be called planets. Some are only the size of a car!

When the solar system formed, small rocks started to clump together. The chunks of rock got bigger. Eventually they formed planets. Asteroids are the leftovers that never became part of a planet. They are found all over the solar system. There are three types of asteroids. Some are rocky, some are metallic, and some have a lot of carbon.

Most asteroids are in the asteroid belt between Mars and Jupiter.

Mars

Jupiter

Trojan asteroids share the orbit of a planet as it moves around the sun.

Asteroid Ida

Some asteroids have their own moons.

If all the asteroids in the solar system clumped together, they would still be smaller than Earth's moon.

GO FIGURE!

There are asteroids called James Bond, Pocahontas, and Sherlock.

Number of asteroids in the asteroid belt: up to 1.9 million that are larger than 0.6 mile (1 kilometer) across

Average distance between asteroids in the asteroid belt: 621,000–1,864,000 miles (1–3 million kilometers)

Number of asteroids with a moon: at least 150

7

VESTA

Vesta is the largest asteroid.
It formed about 4.5 billion years ago.
Vesta lies in the asteroid belt.

Vesta's surface is made of frozen lava. A massive collision about a billion years ago left an enormous crater. Vesta is nearly round, like the planets. But it has long, deep channels around its middle. A lot of what we know about Vesta comes from the Dawn spacecraft.

Dawn

Dawn arrived at Vesta in 2011 and orbited it for more than a year.

Vesta is not the largest object in the asteroid belt. Ceres is bigger, but it is a dwarf planet.

Diameter: 329 miles (530 kilometers)
Length of day: 5.3 Earth hours
Length of year: 3.6 Earth years
Average daytime temperature: –76 ˚F (–60 ˚C)
Largest crater: 310 miles (500 kilometers) wide

Vesta is named for the Roman goddess of the hearth and home.

Many of the meteorites that have landed on Earth are pieces of Vesta.

Iron core

Vesta has layers called the **core**, mantle, and crust—just like Earth.

Mantle

Crust

9

NEAR-EARTH ASTEROIDS

Asteroids have collided with Earth in the past. They might do so again! Astronomers look out for asteroids that travel close to our planet.

Asteroids with orbits fairly close to Earth are called **near-Earth asteroids** (NEAs). Occasionally one comes within tens of thousands of miles of Earth. Even a fairly small asteroid could have a big impact if it hit Earth. Many scientists think that an asteroid crashing into Earth made the dinosaurs die out.

Several **telescopes** on Earth discover and track near-Earth asteroids.

NASA keeps track of all NEAs that are more than 0.6 mile (1 kilometer) wide.

About once a year, a car-sized asteroid gets close to Earth. It burns in the **atmosphere**, creating a fireball.

The **gravity** of planets can affect asteroids and make them change direction.

GO FIGURE!

Estimated number of NEAs: 1,000 that are more than 0.6 miles (1 kilometer) wide

Earth's Vredefort Crater (caused by an asteroid): 118 miles (190 kilometers) wide

Speed of the NEA Eros: 15.2 miles (24.4 kilometers) per second

EROS

Most asteroids are oddly shaped and lumpy. The asteroid Eros certainly fits this description!

Eros was the first near-Earth asteroid to be discovered. It was also the first asteroid to have a spacecraft orbit it and land on it. End to end, it is only 21.4 miles (34.4 kilometers) long. Its small size and mass mean that it has very weak gravity. Eros's orbit sometimes takes it fairly close to Earth.

100 lb

Something that weighs 100 pounds (45 kilograms) on Earth would weigh only 1 ounce (28 grams) on Eros.

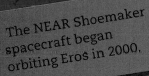

NEAR Shoemaker

The NEAR Shoemaker spacecraft began orbiting Eros in 2000.

Eros was named for the Greek god of love.

GO FIGURE!

Craters spotted by NEAR Shoemaker: 100,000
Photos taken by NEAR Shoemaker: 160,000
Distance from Earth when the spacecraft landed: 196 million miles (315 million kilometers)
Closest recent approach to Earth: 16.6 million miles (26.7 million kilometers)

Eros is about five times larger than the asteroid that hit Earth and killed the dinosaurs.

Because of its odd shape, gravity on Eros is stronger in some parts than others.

COMETS

Humans have watched comets race across the sky for thousands of years. Ancient people thought they were signs from the gods, warning of trouble or death.

Comets are lumps of rock, ice, and dust. Many comets come from a place called the Oort Cloud. This is right at the edge of the solar system. Sometimes gravity pulls a comet into a path around the sun. When a comet gets close to the sun, it warms up and releases gases. The **solar wind** pushes on the gases, forming long, bright tails.

Close-up of a comet's surface

Gas tail

The word "comet" comes from the ancient Greek for "long-haired."

Comets have two tails: one is made of gas and the other of dust.

Dust tail

A comet's tail always points away from the sun, no matter which direction the comet is traveling.

GO FIGURE!

Shortest orbit around the sun: 3 years
Longest orbit: 30 million years (for some Oort Cloud comets)
Halley's Comet orbit: about 76 years
Halley's Comet size: about 9 miles (15 kilometers) wide
Shrinking comet: Halley's diameter shrinks by about 40 feet (12 meters) on each trip around the sun.

A comet called Halley's Comet has been seen many times over the centuries.

INSIDE A COMET

It took a long time for astronomers to confirm what comets are made of. They were helped by a spacecraft that crashed into a comet on purpose!

The main body of a comet is called the **nucleus**. The Deep Impact spacecraft crashed into Comet Tempel 1. It found that the nucleus is made of dust and ice. The surface is covered with black material like soot. As a comet nears the sun, the nucleus warms up. Solid ice turns to gas, forming an atmosphere called a **coma**.

Another spacecraft, called Stardust, collected dust from a comet and brought it back to Earth.

The main body of a comet can be roughly the size of a small town.

Deep Impact sent out a smaller "impactor" that crashed into Comet Tempel 1.

Comet Tempel 1

Deep Impact

GO FIGURE!

Comet Tempel 1 nucleus: 3.73 miles (6 kilometers) wide
Comet Tempel 1 orbit: about 5.56 Earth years
Impactor size: 3.3 feet (1 meter) wide
Impactor weight: 770 pounds (349 kilograms)
Impactor speed: 23,000 miles (37,015 kilometers) per hour

Some ice in comets is frozen water. Comets also have frozen **carbon dioxide**.

COMET SHOEMAKER-LEVY

The solar system is very spread out. Even so, comets sometimes crash into other objects. A comet called Shoemaker-Levy went up against Jupiter—and lost.

Jupiter is the biggest planet in the solar system, and its gravity is very strong. Jupiter captured Comet Shoemaker-Levy, forcing the comet into orbit around it. After several years, Jupiter's gravity tore the comet's nucleus apart. In 1994, the pieces of the comet crashed into Jupiter.

The comet left dark "scars" in Jupiter's clouds. The "scars" were eventually blown away by Jupiter's winds.

Scars

Jupiter

The comet was named for the people who discovered it: Eugene and Carolyn Shoemaker, and David Levy.

The impact was witnessed by the Hubble Space Telescope and other spacecraft.

GO FIGURE!

Size of original comet nucleus:
0.9–1.2 miles (1.5–2 kilometers) wide
Number of fragments: 21
Force of impact: the same as 300 million atomic bombs
Plumes created by the impact:
1,200–1,900 miles (2,000–3,000 kilometers) high

It took a week for all the fragments to crash into Jupiter.

Shoemaker-Levy

ROSETTA

On November 12, 2014, scientists cheered as a tiny spacecraft sent back a signal. It had become the first spacecraft to land on a comet.

The Rosetta mission had two parts. The main spacecraft would study a comet from orbit. A **lander** called Philae would land on the comet's nucleus. Philae had a bumpy landing. It bounced and ended up in a dark crack. There was not enough sunlight to keep its batteries charged. Without power, it could not send back any more information.

The comet studied by Rosetta is called Comet 67P/Churyumov-Gerasimenko.

Rosetta

Two large "wings" of solar panels captured the sun's energy to power the Rosetta spacecraft.

solar panels

Rosetta spent part of the long journey in hibernation mode.

Philae lander

Rosetta was launched in 2004. It took the spacecraft 10 years to reach the comet.

GO FIGURE!

Comet 67P size: about 1.9 by 3.1 miles (3 by 5 kilometers) across
Comet 67P orbit: 6.5 years
Rosetta wingspan: 105 feet (32 meters)
Distance traveled: 4 billion miles (6.4 billion kilometers) to reach the comet
Philae weight: 220 pounds (100 kilograms)

From orbit, Rosetta mapped the comet's surface to choose the best landing site.

METEORS

We sometimes see "shooting stars" streak across the sky. But these are not stars at all. They are space rocks burning up in Earth's atmosphere.

Meteoroids are small pieces of rock in space. Every day, many of these small rocks arrive at Earth. They heat up as they travel through Earth's atmosphere. This creates a glowing trail called a **meteor**. Most rocks burn up completely. A few pass through the atmosphere. The pieces that land on Earth are called meteorites.

A very bright meteor is called a fireball. Some of them explode in the atmosphere.

Meteor

Many meteors are caused by objects no bigger than a grain of sand.

Most meteorites found on Earth are smaller than a fist. A few are much larger.

GO FIGURE!

Mass of meteorites: about 48.5 tons (44,000 kilograms) land on Earth every day
Altitude: most meteors occur between 50 and 75 miles (80 and 120 kilometers) above the ground
Speed: from 25,000 to 160,000 miles per hour (11 to 72 kilometers per second) when entering the atmosphere

Many meteoroids are pieces that once broke off an asteroid.

A fireball in 1908 made a blast that knocked down millions of trees.

METEOR SHOWERS

Sometimes many meteors appear in a short space of time. This amazing sight is called a meteor shower.

Most meteor showers are caused by comets. They happen when Earth travels through a trail of dust left behind by a comet. The pieces of dust burn up in the atmosphere, making meteors. There are several different meteor showers. Each one happens at the same time each year.

Comet dust stays for hundreds of years or more, creating a meteor shower every year.

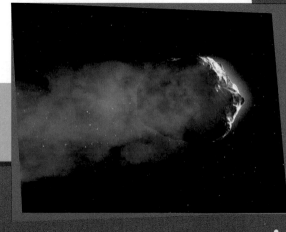